SCHIRMER'S LIBRARY
OF MUSICAL CLASSICS

Vol. 2110

T0066602

PIANO MASTERWORKS

INTERMEDIATE LEVEL

127 Pieces by 24 Composers

ISBN 978-1-4950-0689-0

G. SCHIRMER, Inc.

DISTRIBUTED BY

HAL•LEONARD®
CORPORATION

7777 W. BLUEMOUND RD. P.O. BOX 13819 MILWAUKEE, WI 53213

Copyright © 2016 by G. Schirmer, Inc. (ASCAP) New York, NY
International Copyright Secured. All Rights Reserved.
Warning: Unauthorized reproduction of this publication is
prohibited by Federal law and subject to criminal prosecution.

www.musicsalesclassical.com
www.halleonard.com

CONTENTS

FRÉDÉRIC CHOPIN

MUZIO CLEMENTI

ANTONIO DIABELLI

JAN LADISLAV DUSSEK

EDVARD GRIEG

CORNELIUS GURLITT

GEORGE FRIDERIC HANDEL

(Continued on next page)

FRANZ SCHUBERT

ROBERT SCHUMANN

PYOTR IL'YICH TCHAIKOVSKY

Minuet
in C minor

Composer Unknown
BWV Appendix 121

March
in G Major

Carl Philipp Emanuel Bach
BWV Appendix 124

Invention No. 1
in C Major

Johann Sebastian Bach
BWV 772

Invention No. 2

in C minor

Johann Sebastian Bach
BWV 773

Invention No. 4
in D minor

Johann Sebastian Bach
BWV 775

Invention No. 8
in F Major

Johann Sebastian Bach
BWV 779

Invention No. 10
in G Major

Johann Sebastian Bach
BWV 781

Invention No. 13
in A minor

Johann Sebastian Bach
BWV 784

Invention No. 14
in B-flat Major

Johann Sebastian Bach
BWV 785

Prelude
in C Major
from *The Well-Tempered Clavier*, Book 1

Johann Sebastian Bach
BWV 846

All figures in the fingering which are set above the notes are intended, whether in inner or outer parts, for the right rand; whereas, the figures below the notes are for the left hand. This explanation will suffice to show, in doubtful cases, by which hand any note in the parts is to be played.

Prelude
in D minor

Johann Sebastian Bach
BWV 926

Prelude
in C Major

Johann Sebastian Bach
BWV 924

Allegro moderato (♩ = 104)

Prelude
in F Major

Johann Sebastian Bach
BWV 927

Prelude
in C minor

Johann Sebastian Bach

BWV 934

Bourée

from Lute Suite No. 1 in E minor

Johann Sebastian Bach
BWV 996

Prelude
in C minor

Johann Sebastian Bach
BWV 999

Bagatelle
from 14 Bagatelles

Béla Bartók
Op. 6, No. 4

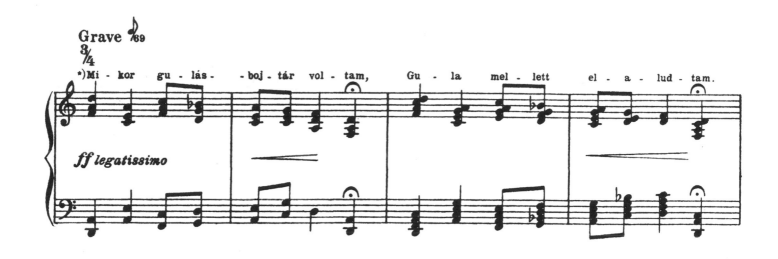

* An old Hungarian folksong from the district west of the Danube. "When I was a cowhand I fell asleep near the cattle.
I awoke about midnight. Not one cow was left."

Six Variations on a Swiss Song

Ludwig van Beethoven
WoO 64

*) We call special attention to these thoroughly delightful Variations because they are far too little known and appreciated. They will be particularly welcome to *young* pianists.

(a) By a comma we mark those points at which the player ought, by lifting his hands a little earlier than the note-value indicates, to bring out a rhythmical division.

(b) Proceed without interrupting the rhythm; and similarly after Variations 1 and 3.

Minore

Poco sostenuto e doloroso (♩ = 112)

Var. III

sempre **p** e legato

Maggiore

Tempo I un poco animato (♩ = 126)

Var. IV

f legato

_5__ Ped. simile

Twelve German Dances

Ludwig van Beethoven
WoO 13

1

2

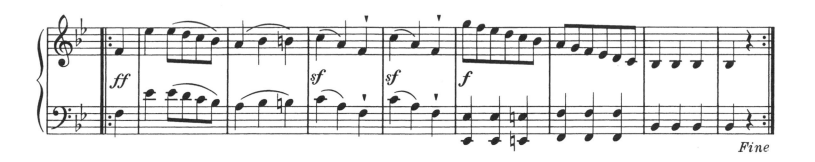

Fine

Trio

D.C.

3

Trio

Fine

Trio

p

D.C.

7

f

sf

sf

Fine

Trio

p

D.C.

8

Fine

Trio

D.C.

9

Fine

Trio

D.C.

10

Fine

Trio

D.C.

11

Fine

Trio

D. C.

12

La chasse

(The Chase)

from *25 Easy and Progressive Studies*

Johann Friedrich Burgmüller
Op. 100, No. 9

Tendre fleur

(Tender Blossom)

from *25 Easy and Progressive Studies*

Johann Friedrich Burgmüller
Op. 100, No. 10

La bergeronnette

(The Wagtail)

from *25 Easy and Progressive Studies*

Johann Friedrich Burgmüller
Op. 100, No. 11

L'adieu

(The Farewell)

from *25 Easy and Progressive Studies*

Johann Friedrich Burgmüller
Op. 100, No. 12

Consolation

from *25 Easy and Progressive Studies*

Johann Friedrich Burgmüller
Op. 100, No.13

Douce plainte

(Tender Grieving)

from *25 Easy and Progressive Studies*

Johann Friedrich Burgmüller
Op. 100, No. 16

La babillarde

(The Chatterbox)

from *25 Easy and Progressive Studies*

Johann Friedrich Burgmüller
Op. 100, No. 17

La tarentelle
(Tarantella)
from *25 Easy and Progressive Studies*

Johann Friedrich Burgmüller
Op. 100, No. 20

Barcarolle

from *25 Easy and Progressive Studies*

Johann Friedrich Burgmüller
Op. 100, No. 22

Le retour

(The Return)

from *25 Easy and Progressive Studies*

Johann Friedrich Burgmüller
Op. 100, No. 23

L'hirondelle

(The Swallow)

from *25 Easy and Progressive Studies*

Johann Friedrich Burgmüller
Op. 100, No. 24

La chevaleresque

(Spirit of Chivalry)

from *25 Easy and Progressive Studies*

Johann Friedrich Burgmüller
Op. 100, No. 25

Study in E Major

Johann Friedrich Burgmüller

from *12 Brilliant and Melodious Studies*

Op. 105, No. 9

Confidence

from *18 Characteristic Studies*

Johann Friedrich Burgmüller
Op. 109, No. 1

Les perles

from *18 Characteristic Studies*

Johann Friedrich Burgmüller
Op. 109, No. 2

Le retour du pâtre

(The Shepherd's Return)

from *18 Characteristic Studies*

Johann Friedrich Burgmüller
Op. 109, No. 3

Agitato

from *18 Characteristic Studies*

Johann Friedrich Burgmüller
Op. 109, No. 8

77

La cloche des matines

(The Matin Bell)

from *18 Characteristic Studies*

Johann Friedrich Burgmüller
Op. 109, No. 9

La vélocité

(Velocity)

from *18 Characteristic Studies*

Johann Friedrich Burgmüller
Op. 109, No. 10

L'orage
(The Storm)
from *18 Characteristic Studies*

Johann Friedrich Burgmüller
Op. 109, No. 13

This étude may serve as an introduction to the next.

Berceuse

(Lullaby)

from *18 Characteristic Studies*

Johann Friedrich Burgmüller
Op. 109, No. 7

Andantino con moto (♪ = 112)

à J. C. Kessler

Prélude
in E minor

Frédéric Chopin
Op. 28, No. 4

à J. C. Kessler

Prélude
in B minor

Frédéric Chopin
Op. 28, No. 6

à J. C. Kessler

Prélude
in A minor

Frédéric Chopin
Op. 28, No. 7

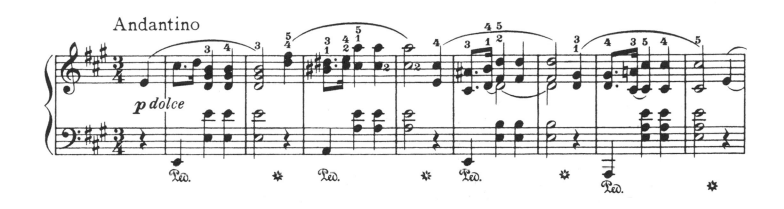

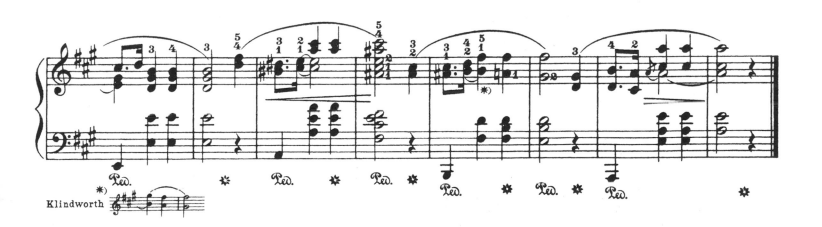

Klindworth

Sonatina
in F Major

Muzio Clementi
Op. 36, No. 4

Andante con espressione

Rondo
Allegro vivace

Da Capo al Fine

Sonatina
in C major

Anton Diabelli
Op. 168, No. 3

Allegro moderato

a)

Rondo

Allegro

Sonatina
in G Major

Jan Ladislav Dussek
Op. 20, No 1

Allegro non tanto

Rondo.
Allegretto Tempo di Minuetto

Waltz
in A minor
from *Lyric Pieces*

Edvard Grieg
Op. 12, No. 2

Coda

Elves' Dance

from *Lyric Pieces*

Edvard Grieg
Op. 12, No. 4

Molto Allegro e sempre staccato

Album Leaf

from *Lyric Pieces*

Edvard Grieg
Op. 12, No. 7

Little Bird
from *Lyric Pieces*

Edvard Grieg
Op. 43, No. 4

Bell Ringing

from *Lyric Pieces*

Edvard Grieg
Op. 54, No. 6

Arietta

from *Lyric Pieces*

Edvard Grieg
Op. 12, No. 1

Poco Andante e sostenuto

Puck
from *Lyric Pieces*

Edvard Grieg
Op. 71, No. 3

The Little Wanderer

from *Albumleaves for the Young*

Cornelius Gurlitt
Op. 101, No. 12

Hunting Song

from *Albumleaves for the Young*

Cornelius Gurlitt
Op. 101, No. 19

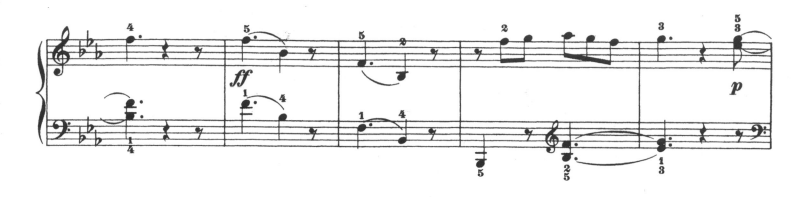

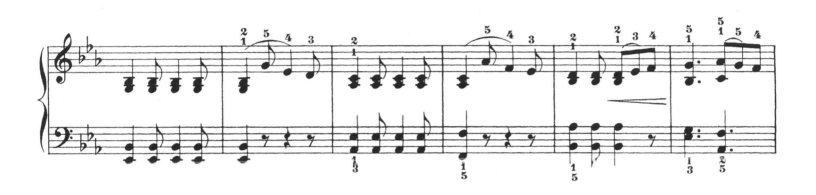

Air con variazioni
from Suite in B-flat Major

George Frideric Handel
HWV 434

Var. V.

Allegro
from Suite in G minor

la 2da volta un poco rit.
George Frideric Handel
HWV 432

The Brook
from *25 Melodious Etudes*

Stephen Heller
Op. 45, No. 1

The Avalanche

from *25 Melodious Etudes*

Stephen Heller
Op. 45, No. 2

Sorrow and Joy

from *25 Melodious Etudes*

Stephen Heller
Op. 45, No. 4

Autumn Song
from *25 Etudes for Piano*

Stephen Heller
Op. 47, No. 3

Allegretto con moto (♩. = 100)

In Venice

from *25 Etudes for Piano*

Stephen Heller
Op. 47, No. 14

Allegretto con moto. (♩. = 80)

Sonatina
in C Major

Friedrich Kuhlau
Op. 55, No. 1

*) Remark: These small slurs indicate that the last bass-note in one measure should be carefully connected with the first bass-note in the next.

On the Playground

from *Scenes from Childhood*

Theodor Kullak
Op. 62, No. 4

Grandmother Tells a Ghost Story

from *Scenes from Childhood*

Theodor Kullak
Op. 81, No. 3

Allegretto

Sonatina
in C Major

Heinrich Lichner
Op. 49, No 1

Allegro moderato (♩ = 132)

Sonatina
in C Major

Heinrich Lichner
Op. 4, No. 1

Allegro moderato (♩ = 132)

Andante cantabile (♩ = 184)

Rondo grazioso
Allegro (♩ = 112)

153

to A. Siloti

Farewell*

Franz Liszt

*Russian folk song

Gray Clouds

Franz Liszt

To a Wild Rose
from *Woodland Sketches*

Edward MacDowell
Op. 51, No. 1

Song Without Words
in A Major

Felix Mendelssohn
Op. 19, No. 4

Song Without Words

in E Major

Felix Mendelssohn
Op. 30, No. 3

Adagio non troppo (♩ = 58)

Song Without Words
in C Major

Felix Mendelssohn
Op. 102, No. 3

Suite No. 6
in D Major

Henry Purcell

Prelude
Moderato

Almand
Andante

Hornpipe
Moderato

*) omit
a) or ⁀

Suite No. 8
in F Major

Henry Purcell

Prelude
Animato

Almand
Molto moderato

* = omit.   a) trill from above in similar places:

Hornpipe
Animato

Minuet

Suite No. 1
in G Major

Henry Purcell

Courante
Moderato

poco mosso

a tempo

a)
or: In similar cases may be omitted or abbreviated.

Minuet

★ may be omitted

Scherzo
in B-flat Major
from *2 Scherzos*

Franz Schubert
D. 593

Allegretto

Fine

Trio

legato

Ped. simile

Ped. simile

Scherzo D.C.

Von fremden Ländern und Menschen

(About Strange Lands and People)

from *Scenes from Childhood*

Robert Schumann
Op. 15, No. 1

Knecht Ruprecht*

from *Album for the Young*

Robert Schumann
Op. 68, No. 12

*English folk-lore has no equivalent for this legendary character, a rough fellow who makes his appearance at Christmas time and takes the children to task for their behavior during the past year.

Fremder Mann
(Strange Man)
from *Album for the Young*

Robert Schumann
Op. 68, No. 29

Kleiner Morgenwanderer

(Roaming in the Morning)

from *Album for the Young*

Robert Schumann
Op. 68, No. 17

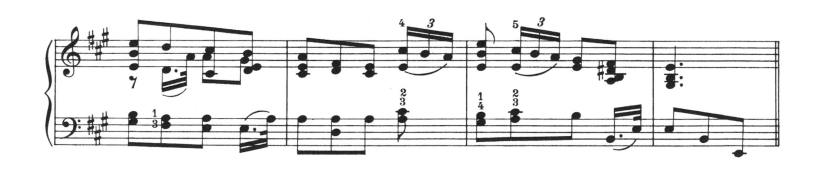

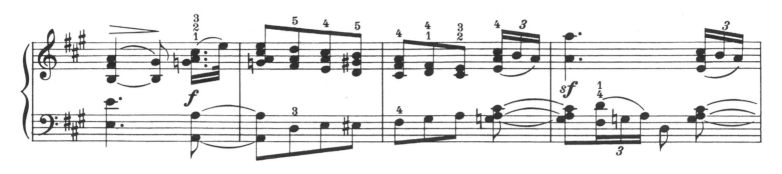

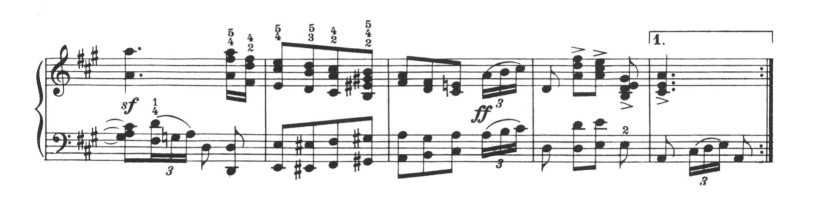

Kleine Romanze
(Little Romance)
from *Album for the Young*

Robert Schumann
Op. 68, No. 19

Lento espressivo*

from *Album for the Young*

Robert Schumann
Op. 68, No. 21

*In the original this piece is headed by three stars: ✱ ✱ ✱

Reiterstücke

(The Horseman)

from *Album for the Young*

Robert Schumann
Op. 68, No. 23

Nachklänge aus dem Theater

(Echoes from the Theatre)

from *Album for the Young*

Robert Schumann
Op. 68, No. 25

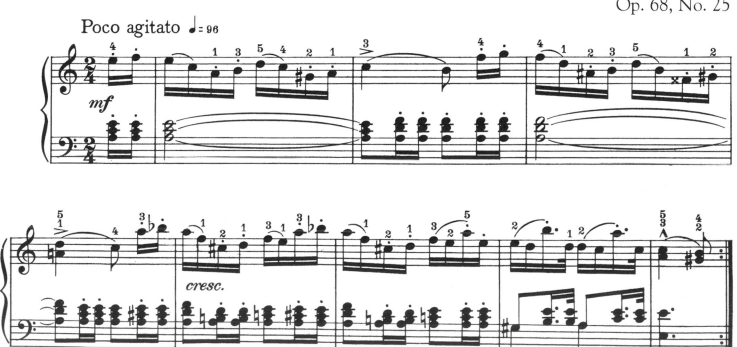

Winterzeit I
(Winter-time I)
from *Album for the Young*

Robert Schumann
Op. 68, No. 38

Little Lullaby

from *Albumleaves*

Robert Schumann
Op. 124, No. 6

Mamma

from *Album for the Young*

Pyotr Il'yich Tchaikovsky
Op. 39, No. 4

March of the Tin Soldiers

from *Album for the Young*

Pyotr Il'yich Tchaikovsky
Op. 39, No. 5

Tempo di Marcia

Mazurka
in D minor
from *Album for the Young*

Pyotr Il'yich Tchaikovsky
Op. 39, No. 10

Tempo di Mazurka

Russian Song

from *Album for the Young*

Pyotr Il'yich Tchaikovsky
Op. 39, No. 11

The Peasant Plays the Accordion

from *Album for the Young*

Pyotr Il'yich Tchaikovsky
Op. 39, No. 12

Italian Song

from *Album for the Young*

Pyotr Il'yich Tchaikovsky
Op. 39, No. 15

Neapolitan Dance Song

from *Album for the Young*

Pyotr Il'yich Tchaikovsky
Op. 39, No. 18

Più mosso

Sweet Dreams

from *Album for the Young*

Pyotr Il'yich Tchaikovsky
Op. 39, No. 21

Song of the Lark

from *Album for the Young*

Pyotr Il'yich Tchaikovsky
Op. 39, No. 22

German Song

from *Album for the Young*

Pyotr Il'yich Tchaikovsky
Op. 39, No. 17

The Organ Grinder

from *Album for the Young*

Pyotr Il'yich Tchaikovsky
Op. 39, No. 23